TRAVEL BOOK SEVILLE

SPAIN 2023

Seville on a Budget: How to Experience
Luxury without Spending a Fortune

Eric J. Richardson

Table Of Contents

Introduction to Seville

Welcome to Seville, the heart of Andalusia and one of Spain's most beautiful and enchanting cities! As a first-time traveler, you're in for a treat, as Seville is a destination that offers something for everyone - from its rich history and culture to its delicious food and wine, to its lively nightlife and entertainment.

Upon arrival, you'll be greeted by a city that is steeped in history and tradition, yet also vibrant and modern. You'll notice the striking architecture of its landmarks, such as the stunning Alcázar of Seville and the towering Seville Cathedral, both of which are must-see attractions. You'll also be struck by the beauty of the winding streets and alleyways of the Santa Cruz neighborhood, with its quaint squares and hidden courtyards that are perfect for getting lost in.

Throughout your stay, you can expect to be delighted by the warmth and hospitality of the Sevillanos, who are known for their friendliness and welcoming nature. You'll have plenty of opportunities to experience this firsthand, whether it's through a conversation with a local over a cup of coffee, or by taking part in the city's many festivals and celebrations, such as the famous Feria de Abril.

Food is a big part of the Sevillian experience, and you'll soon discover the joys of tapas - small, savory dishes that are perfect for sharing with friends over a glass of wine or a cold beer. You'll find plenty of tapas bars throughout the city, serving up everything from classic Spanish tortillas to local specialties like salmorejo, a delicious cold soup made with tomatoes and bread.

Finally, Seville is a city that loves to party, and you'll find plenty of opportunities to do just that, whether it's dancing the night away at a flamenco show or hitting up one of the city's many bars and clubs. Whatever your interests, Seville is sure to capture your heart and leave you with memories that will last a lifetime. So sit back, relax, and prepare to fall in love with this lovely city.

About Seville

History

Seville is a city with a long and fascinating history, dating back over 2,000 years. Founded as the Roman city of Hispalis, Seville was an important trading hub and military outpost for the Romans, who built many of the city's most enduring landmarks, including the aqueduct and the nearby Roman ruins of Italica.

Following the fall of the Roman Empire, Seville was ruled by various Visigothic and Islamic dynasties, who left their mark on the city's architecture, art, and culture. In the 8th century, Seville was captured by the Moors, who made it the capital of their Al-Andalus region and transformed it into a center of learning, trade, and the arts.

During this time, Seville was a crossroads of cultures, with Christians, Jews, and Muslims living side by side in relative harmony. It was during this period that many of Seville's most iconic landmarks were built, including the Giralda Tower, which was originally a minaret, and the Alcázar, a stunning palace complex that still stands today.

In the 13th century, Seville was conquered by the Christian armies of King Ferdinand III, who established the city as a center of power for the newly-united Kingdom of Castile and Leon. Under Christian rule, Seville became an important center of commerce and exploration, with Spanish conquistadors such as Hernando Cortes setting out from Seville to conquer the New World.

Throughout the centuries that followed, Seville continued to grow and prosper, with new landmarks such as the Seville Cathedral and the Plaza de España being built during the 15th and 16th centuries. Seville's rich cultural heritage was also celebrated during this time, with the city becoming a hub of the Spanish Baroque movement and a center of flamenco music and dance.

Today, Seville remains one of Spain's most beloved cities, celebrated for its rich history, stunning architecture, and vibrant culture. Visitors to the city can explore its many landmarks, sample its delicious cuisine, and experience the warmth and hospitality of its people, all while immersing themselves in the fascinating history of this ancient city.

Culture

Seville is a city with a vibrant culture, shaped by centuries of history and influenced by its diverse mix of peoples and traditions. From its architecture and art to its cuisine and music, Seville is a city that celebrates its heritage while embracing the new.

One of the most important aspects of Sevillian culture is its love of flamenco, a traditional style of music and dance that originated in Andalusia. Flamenco is an integral part of Sevillian life, with many locals performing and enjoying the art form regularly. Visitors to the city can experience flamenco in its many forms, from intimate performances in traditional bars and clubs to large-scale shows at the city's many theaters and venues.

Seville is also famous for its food, with a cuisine that is deeply rooted in local traditions and ingredients. From tapas bars serving up small, savory dishes to seafood restaurants specializing in fresh fish caught off the nearby coast, Seville's culinary scene is a feast for the senses. Some of the city's most beloved dishes include gazpacho, a refreshing cold soup made with tomatoes and vegetables, and tortilla de Camarones, a crispy shrimp fritter that is a local specialty.

The city's architecture is another important part of its cultural heritage, with many of its most iconic landmarks reflecting the influence of the Moors, who ruled the city for centuries. The Alcázar, for example, is a stunning palace complex that blends Gothic and Islamic styles, while the Giralda Tower, once a minaret, is now a bell tower that offers panoramic views of the city. Other notable landmarks include the Seville Cathedral, one of the largest Gothic cathedrals in the world, and the Plaza de España, a grand square built for the 1929 World's Fair.

Finally, Seville is a city that loves to celebrate, with a calendar full of festivals and events throughout the year. The Semana Santa, or Holy Week, is one of the city's most important religious festivals, while the

Feria de Abril is a week-long celebration of music, dance, and culture that takes place in April. Other festivals include the Dia de los Reyes Magos, or Three Kings' Day, and the Dia de la Cruz, a colorful celebration of the city's neighborhoods and communities.

All of these elements come together to create a rich and diverse cultural landscape that is uniquely Sevillian. Seville is a city that has something for everyone, whether you're exploring the city's architecture, tasting its food, or immersing yourself in its music and dance.

Geography and Climate

Seville is located in the southern region of Spain known as Andalusia and is situated along the banks of the Guadalquivir River. The city is surrounded by a fertile plain known as the Vega de Sevilla, which is home to many of the region's crops, including olives, oranges, and sunflowers.

The climate of Seville is Mediterranean, with long, hot summers and mild, rainy winters. The city experiences more than 3,000 hours of sunshine per year, making it one of the sunniest cities in Europe. Summers are typically dry and very hot, with temperatures often reaching 40°C (104°F) or higher. Winters are mild and rainy, with temperatures rarely dropping below freezing.

The weather in Seville is influenced by its location in the interior of Andalusia, as well as its proximity to the Atlantic Ocean and the Mediterranean Sea. The hot, dry summers are a result of the city's inland location, while the mild winters are due to the influence of the Atlantic and Mediterranean winds. Despite the hot temperatures, Seville is a city that can be enjoyed year-round, with many indoor attractions and activities available to escape the heat during the summer months. Spring and fall are popular times to visit, as temperatures are milder and many festivals and events take place during these seasons. Overall, Seville's geography and climate make it a unique and fascinating destination, with a sunny and warm atmosphere that is sure to delight visitors from around the world.

Overview of Seville Neighborhoods

Seville is a city with a rich and diverse urban landscape, characterized by a mix of historic neighborhoods, modern developments, and green spaces. Each neighborhood in Seville has its distinct character, with unique architecture, attractions, and local flavor. In this article, we'll take a closer look at some of the most popular neighborhoods in Seville and what makes each one special.

Santa Cruz

One of the most iconic neighborhoods in Seville, Santa Cruz is located in the historic center of the city and is known for its narrow, winding streets and charming architecture. Once the Jewish quarter of the city, Santa Cruz is now a popular destination for visitors, with many restaurants, bars, and shops nestled in its narrow alleys and plazas. The neighborhood is also home to many of Seville's most important landmarks, including the Seville Cathedral and the Alcázar Palace complex.

Triana

Located across the Guadalquivir River from the historic center of Seville, Triana is a neighborhood with a strong cultural identity and a rich history. Known for its ceramics, flamenco, and traditional tapas bars, Triana is a lively and vibrant neighborhood that offers a glimpse into Seville's authentic local culture. The streets of Triana are lined with colorful buildings, while the riverside promenade offers stunning views of the city's skyline.

Macarena

The Macarena neighborhood is located to the north of the historic center of Seville and is known for its bohemian vibe and eclectic mix of attractions. The neighborhood is home to many cultural institutions, including the Andalusian Center for Contemporary Art and the Basilica of the Macarena, which houses the famous statue of the Virgin of Hope. The streets of the Macarena are lined with vintage boutiques, independent cafes, and trendy bars, making it a popular destination for young people and creative types.

Alameda

Located just outside the historic center of Seville, the Alameda neighborhood is a hip and trendy district that is popular with locals and visitors alike.

The neighborhood is centered around the Alameda de Hercules, a large public square that is lined with restaurants, bars, and cafes. The Alameda is also home to many of Seville's cultural institutions, including the Teatro Alameda and the Contemporary Art Center. The streets of Alameda are lined with colorful street art, making it a popular destination for art lovers and Instagrammers.

La Cartuja

Located to the west of the city center, La Cartuja is a modern development that was built for the 1992 World's Fair. The neighborhood is known for its innovative architecture and futuristic design, with many of its buildings featuring striking shapes and bold colors. La Cartuja is also home to many cultural institutions, including the Andalusian Contemporary Art Center and the Science Museum. The neighborhood is a popular destination for families and those interested in modern architecture and design.

Nervión

Located to the east of the city center, Nervión is a modern and well-connected neighborhood that is popular with business travelers and expats. The neighborhood is home to many high-rise buildings, as well as the city's main train station and several large shopping centers. Despite its modern feel, Nervión is also home to many green spaces, including the expansive Maria Luisa Park.

These are just a few of the many neighborhoods that make Seville such a unique and fascinating city. Each neighborhood has its distinct character, with unique attractions, architecture, and local flavor. Whether you're looking to explore the historic center, soak up the local culture, or immerse yourself in modern design and architecture, Seville has something for everyone.

Why Seville is a popular travel destination

Seville is a popular travel destination for people from all over the world and for good reason. This vibrant city in southern Spain is known for its rich history, beautiful architecture, delicious food, and lively culture. Let's take a closer look at why Seville is such a popular travel destination and what makes it a must-visit city.

Rich History and Architecture
Seville has a long and rich history that is reflected in its stunning architecture and historic landmarks. The city was founded by the Romans, and over the centuries it was ruled by various cultures, including the Moors and the Christians. This diverse history is

reflected in the city's architecture, which features a mix of Roman, Gothic, Renaissance, and Islamic styles.

One of the most iconic landmarks in Seville is the Cathedral of Saint Mary of the See, also known as the Seville Cathedral. This magnificent cathedral is the largest Gothic cathedral in the world and is home to the tomb of Christopher Columbus. Other notable landmarks in Seville include the Alcázar palace complex, the Giralda bell tower, and the Plaza de España, a grand square built for the 1929 Ibero-American Exposition.

Lively Culture and Festivals

Seville is known for its lively culture, with a vibrant arts scene, traditional flamenco music and dance, and delicious cuisine. The city is also famous for its festivals, which are held throughout the year and attract visitors from all over the world.

One of the most popular festivals in Seville is the Feria de Abril, a week-long celebration held in April that features colorful parades, traditional dress, and plenty of food and drink. Another popular festival is the Semana Santa, or Holy Week, which takes place in the lead-up to Easter and is marked by processions, religious ceremonies, and traditional music.

Delicious Food and Wine

Seville is also known for its delicious food and wine, with a rich culinary tradition that is influenced by both Spanish and Moorish cuisine. Some of the most popular dishes in Seville include tapas, small plates of food that are perfect for sharing and trying a variety of different flavors. Some of the most popular tapas in Seville include fried fish, tortilla española (a type of potato omelet), and croquetas (small balls of fried dough filled with ham or cheese).

Seville is also known for its excellent wine, with several wine regions located nearby. Some of the most popular wines in Seville include Rioja, Ribera del Duero, and Jerez, the latter of which is also used to make sherry.

Beautiful Parks and Gardens

In addition to its rich history, culture, and cuisine, Seville is also known for its beautiful parks and gardens. One of the most famous parks in Seville is Maria Luisa Park, a sprawling green space that is home to several museums, fountains, and monuments. The park is also home to the Plaza de España, a grand square built for the 1929 Ibero-American Exposition.

Another beautiful green space in Seville is the Alcazar Gardens, located within the Alcázar palace complex. These stunning gardens feature a mix of

Islamic and Renaissance styles, with fountains, courtyards, and beautifully manicured lawns.

Accessibility and Transportation
Seville is also a popular travel destination because of its accessibility and transportation options. The city is served by Seville Airport, which offers regular flights to destinations throughout Europe. The city is also well-connected by train and bus, making it easy to explore other parts of Spain.

Within Seville itself, the city is relatively easy to navigate by foot, with many of the main attractions located within walking distance of each other. The city also has a comprehensive public transportation system, including buses, trams, and a metro line, making it easy to get around the city quickly and affordably.

Low Cost of Living

One of the reasons Seville is such a popular travel destination is its low cost of living. Compared to other cities in Europe, Seville is relatively inexpensive, making it an ideal destination for budget-conscious travelers. Accommodation, food, and transportation are all reasonably priced, making it easy to enjoy all that Seville has to offer without breaking the bank.

Whether you're interested in history, art, food, or simply soaking up the vibrant atmosphere of a lively Spanish city, Seville is sure to offer something for everyone.

Chapter1: Planning Your Trip to Seville

Best time to visit Seville

Seville is a beautiful city located in the southern part of Spain and is a popular destination for tourists throughout the year. However, the best time to visit Seville largely depends on your preferences and travel plans. In this article, we'll take a closer look at the climate and peak travel seasons in Seville to help you decide when to plan your visit.

Climate

Seville has a Mediterranean climate with hot, dry summers and mild, rainy winters. The city experiences a significant temperature difference between summer and winter, with temperatures reaching as high as 40°C (104°F) in the summer and dropping to around 10°C (50°F) in the winter.

The best time to visit Seville is generally in the spring (March to May) and autumn (September to November), when the weather is mild and comfortable. During these months, temperatures typically range from 18-28°C (64-82°F) during the day and around 10-18°C (50-64°F) at night. The spring is particularly beautiful in Seville, with blooming orange trees and flowers adding to the city's charm.

Summer (June to August) in Seville can be very hot and humid, with temperatures often reaching above 35°C (95°F) during the day. This can make sightseeing and outdoor activities difficult and uncomfortable, especially during the middle of the day. If you do decide to visit Seville in the summer, be sure to take plenty of precautions to stay cool and hydrated, such as carrying a water bottle and wearing light, breathable clothing.

Winter (December to February) in Seville is mild but can be rainy, with average temperatures ranging from 8-17°C (46-63°F). While the winter is not as popular a time to visit Seville as the spring or autumn, it can be a good option for travelers looking to avoid crowds and enjoy lower prices.

Peak Travel Seasons

Seville is a popular travel destination all year round, but the city experiences peak travel seasons during certain times of the year. These peak seasons are typically associated with major holidays and festivals in Seville, as well as school vacations in other parts of Europe.

The two busiest times of year to visit Seville are during the Semana Santa (Holy Week) and the Feria de Abril (April Fair). Semana Santa is a religious festival that takes place in the week leading up to Easter, and the Feria de Abril is a week-long celebration that takes place two weeks after Semana Santa. During both of these events, Seville is filled with locals and tourists alike, and accommodation prices can be very high.

If you're planning to visit Seville during Semana Santa or the Feria de Abril, it's important to book your accommodation and travel arrangements well in advance. Keep in mind that many businesses and attractions may also have limited hours or be closed during these festivals, so it's a good idea to plan your itinerary accordingly.

Other peak travel seasons in Seville include the summer months, especially July and August, when many European tourists are on summer vacation, and the winter holidays, including Christmas and New Year's Eve. If you plan to visit Seville during these times, be prepared for higher prices and larger crowds.

Off-Peak Travel Seasons

If you're looking to avoid the crowds and high prices of peak travel seasons in Seville, consider visiting during the shoulder seasons. These are the periods just before or after the peak seasons when the weather is still pleasant but the crowds have thinned out.

In Seville, the shoulder seasons are generally the spring and autumn months, except the weeks surrounding Semana Santa and the Feria de Abril. During these times, you can still enjoy the mild weather and many of the city's attractions without dealing with large crowds or inflated prices.

Another option for off-peak travel is the winter season, especially January and February. While it may be chillier and rainier during these months, you'll likely find fewer tourists and lower prices on accommodation and flights.

Overall, the best time to visit Seville depends on your priorities and travel preferences. If you want to experience the city's biggest festivals and don't mind the crowds and higher prices, consider visiting during Semana Santa or the Feria de Abril. If you're looking for pleasant weather and smaller crowds, plan your visit for the spring or autumn. And if you're on a budget and don't mind cooler weather, the winter season may be the perfect time to explore Seville.

No matter when you visit Seville, you're sure to find a beautiful city filled with history, culture, and stunning architecture. From the famous Alcázar and Cathedral to the charming neighborhoods and delicious food, there's something for everyone in Seville. Just be sure to plan your trip and pack accordingly for the weather, and you're sure to have a wonderful time in this amazing city.

How to get to Seville

Seville is a beautiful city in the south of Spain and is a popular destination for tourists from all over the world. The city is well-connected, with several transportation options available for visitors to reach it. In this article, we will explore the different ways to get to Seville, as well as the transportation options available to get around the city.

By Air:

Seville has its airport, San Pablo Airport (SVQ), which is located approximately 10 kilometers (6 miles) from the city center. The airport serves several airlines, including Ryanair, Vueling, and Iberia, and offers direct flights to several destinations in Europe. Once you arrive at the airport, you can take a taxi, bus, or rental car to reach the city center.

The airport has several transportation options for visitors. The most convenient option is to take a taxi, which takes about 20 minutes to reach the city center and costs around €25-€35, depending on your destination. Alternatively, you can take a bus from the airport to the city center. The bus departs every 30 minutes and costs around €4 per person. Another option is to rent a car, which can be done at the airport. There are several rental car companies available, and it is recommended to book in advance to ensure availability and to get the best rates.

By Train:

Seville has a high-speed train station, Santa Justa, which is located in the city center and is well-connected to several cities in Spain, including Madrid, Barcelona, Malaga, and Valencia. The train station is operated by Renfe, the national train company in Spain. You can book your tickets online or at the station, and there are several trains available throughout the day.

The high-speed train is the most popular option for visitors who are traveling from other cities in Spain. The train is fast, comfortable, and offers beautiful views of the countryside. The journey from Madrid to Seville takes approximately 2.5 hours, and from Barcelona to Seville takes approximately 5 hours.

By Bus:

Seville has a modern bus station, Estación de Autobuses Plaza de Armas, which is located in the city center and offers connections to several destinations in Spain and Portugal. Major bus companies such as ALSA, Avanza, and Alsa Premium operate from this station, and you can book tickets online or at the station.

The bus is a convenient and affordable option for visitors who are traveling from other cities in Spain. The journey from Madrid to Seville takes approximately 6 hours, and from Barcelona to Seville takes approximately 12 hours. The bus station is well-connected to the city center, and you can take a taxi or bus to reach your destination.

By Car:

Seville is well-connected by road and is easily accessible by car. The city has several highways that connect it to other major cities in Spain, including the A-4, A-49, and A-92. If you plan to rent a car, make sure to book in advance to get the best rates. Seville has several rental car companies available, including Avis, Europcar, and Hertz.

Other parts of Europe and the World

Air travel is the most common way to get to Seville from other parts of the world. The city's international airport, Seville Airport (SVQ), is located just 10 kilometers from the city center and is served by several airlines, including budget carriers like Ryanair and EasyJet. Direct flights to Seville are available from major cities across Europe, including London, Paris, Berlin, Amsterdam, and Dublin, as well as from some destinations in North Africa.

If you are traveling from outside of Europe, you may need to connect through another European city to reach Seville. Major airlines like British Airways, Lufthansa, and Air France offer connecting flights to Seville through their hubs in London, Frankfurt, and Paris, respectively. Depending on your point of origin, you may also be able to find direct or connecting flights to Seville through smaller airlines or charter companies.

If you are traveling from other parts of Spain or Europe, another option is to take the train to Seville. The city is served by several high-speed trains, including the AVE, which connects Seville to Madrid in just over two hours. Other destinations that can be reached by train from Seville include

Barcelona, Valencia, and Malaga, among others. Train travel in Spain is generally comfortable and reliable, and the scenery along many routes is beautiful.

If you prefer to drive, Seville is well-connected to other parts of Spain by an extensive network of highways. The city is located about two hours by car from Madrid, and about three and a half hours from Valencia. If you are driving from Portugal, Seville is about two hours from the border. While driving in Spain can be enjoyable, it is important to note that traffic can be heavy in major cities like Seville, especially during peak travel periods.

Once you have arrived in Seville, there are several transportation options to help you get around the city. Public transportation is affordable and reliable, with buses and trams serving most parts of the city. Taxis are also readily available and can be hailed on the street or called in advance. If you prefer to explore the city on foot or by bike, several companies offer bike rentals, as well as walking and cycling tours.

Getting Around Seville

Overview of transportation options within Seville Seville is a vibrant and bustling city that attracts millions of tourists each year, and as such, it's important to know how to get around the city. Fortunately, Seville has a well-developed public transportation system that is efficient and affordable for visitors. In addition to public transportation, taxis are readily available, and cycling and walking are popular ways to explore the city.

Public transportation

One of the most popular ways to get around Seville is by using the city's metro system, called

MetroSevilla. The metro operates two lines that connect most of the city's major tourist sites and neighborhoods.

The first line, Line 1, runs from Ciudad Expo to Olivar de Quintos and stops at popular tourist attractions such as the Plaza de España, the Cathedral, and the Alcazar. The second line, Line 2, runs from Ciudad Expo to the Seville Santa Justa railway station and connects the city center to the suburbs. Both lines are efficient and provide a fast and convenient way to get around Seville.

In addition to the metro, Seville also has an extensive bus network that operates throughout the city and to some of the surrounding towns. The buses are inexpensive and provide an excellent way to get around Seville and see the sights. The bus network is operated by the company Tussam, and the buses are modern and air-conditioned, making them a comfortable way to travel.

One of the benefits of using the bus system in Seville is the ability to purchase a rechargeable card called the Tarjeta Multi, which can be used on both the bus and the metro. The card can be purchased at any metro station or bus stop and is a convenient way to pay for transportation in Seville.

Taxis

Taxis are also readily available in Seville and can be hailed on the street or booked in advance. Taxis are a bit more expensive than public transportation, but they are still affordable and provide a convenient way to get around the city. It's important to keep in mind that taxi fares can increase during peak hours and late at night. Taxis in Seville are regulated by the local government, and as such, the fares are fixed and cannot be negotiated.

Cycling

Another popular transportation option in Seville is cycling. There are numerous bike rental shops throughout the city, and Seville has over 170 kilometers of bike lanes, making it one of the most bike-friendly cities in Europe. Renting a bike is a great way to explore the city at your own pace, and many of the top tourist sites in Seville are easily accessible by bike.

There are several bike rental companies in Seville, and most of them offer guided tours of the city, which can be a great way to learn about the city's history and culture while exploring it on two wheels. It's important to keep in mind that cycling in Seville can be challenging, particularly during peak traffic hours, so it's important to follow the rules of the road and wear a helmet.

Walking

Finally, walking is always an option in Seville, particularly in the city center, which is filled with pedestrian streets and charming plazas. Walking is a great way to get a feel for the city and experience its unique ambiance. It's important to wear comfortable shoes, particularly during the summer months when temperatures can be high.

One of the benefits of walking in Seville is the ability to discover hidden gems and charming neighborhoods that are off the beaten path. The city's historic center is filled with narrow streets and alleyways that are perfect for exploring on foot, and many of the city's top tourist sites are located within walking distance of each other.

Getting to and from the airport:

Seville has a modern international airport, located around 10 kilometers from the city center. There are several transportation options available for travelers arriving at or departing from the airport. The most convenient option is a taxi, which can be hailed outside the airport terminal or booked in advance using a taxi app. Alternatively, there is a bus service that connects the airport with the city center, with several stops along the way. The bus runs from early morning until late at night, and tickets can be purchased onboard or at the airport.

With its efficient public transportation system and pedestrian-friendly streets, Seville is a great city to explore, no matter how you choose to

Tips for navigating Seville's narrow streets and alleyways

Seville's historic center is known for its narrow streets and charming alleyways, which are a testament to the city's rich history and culture. While these streets and alleys are part of Seville's unique charm, they can also be challenging to navigate for visitors, particularly those who are not used to walking on narrow streets.

Here are some tips for navigating Seville's narrow streets and alleyways:

Wear comfortable shoes: Seville's historic center is best explored on foot, so it's important to wear comfortable shoes. Many of the streets and alleys are cobblestoned, which can make walking uncomfortable if you're wearing the wrong shoes. Flat, sturdy shoes with good support are recommended.

Use a map or GPS: Seville's historic center can be confusing to navigate, and it's easy to get lost in the maze of streets and alleys. Using a map or GPS can help you stay on track and find your way around. Many of the streets and alleys are not labeled, so it's important to have a good sense of direction.

Take your time: Seville's historic center is not a place to rush through. Take your time to explore the streets and alleys, and enjoy the architecture, colors, and smells of the city. It's easy to miss hidden gems if you're in a hurry.

Be aware of your surroundings: Seville's narrow streets and alleys can be crowded, particularly during peak tourist season. Be aware of your surroundings and keep an eye out for pickpockets or other potential dangers. It's always a good idea to keep your valuables close and be cautious of strangers.

Follow the locals: The locals know Seville's streets and alleys better than anyone, so it's a good idea to follow their lead. If you see locals walking in a certain direction, they are likely taking the most direct route to their destination.

Take breaks: Seville's narrow streets and alleys can be overwhelming, particularly if you're not used to walking in such close quarters. Take breaks often to rest and recharge, and take in the sights and sounds of the city.

Watch out for traffic: While many of Seville's streets and alleys are pedestrian-only, some are shared with vehicles. Be aware of traffic and stay alert when crossing streets or walking near vehicles.

By following these tips, you can make the most of your time in Seville's historic center and enjoy all that the city has to offer.

Information on other alternative transportation options

Horse Carriages:

Taking a horse carriage ride through the historic center of Seville is a unique and romantic way to see the city. These carriages are usually found in tourist hotspots, such as the Cathedral and the Plaza de España, and can accommodate up to four people. The drivers, or coaches, will take you on a guided tour of the city, pointing out landmarks and sharing interesting historical information about Seville. The prices for horse carriage rides are usually fixed and vary depending on the length of the ride.

Scooters:

Scooter rentals are a popular and convenient way to explore Seville. Lime and Bird are two popular scooter rental companies that offer electric scooters that can be picked up and dropped off at designated locations throughout the city. These scooters are perfect for short trips around the city and are easy to park in narrow streets and alleys. They are a great way to cover more ground and see more of the city than you would on foot.

Segway Tours:

Segway tours are a fun and unique way to explore Seville's narrow streets and alleys. Segways are personal transportation devices that use gyroscopic technology to balance the rider as they move forward and backward. Several companies offer guided Segway tours of the city, including Segway Tour Seville and Seville Segway Tours.

These tours are usually led by a guide who will take you on a route through the city, stopping at key landmarks and points of interest along the way. Segway tours are a great way to cover more ground and see more of the city than you would on foot, while still being eco-friendly and easy to use.

These options are also a great way to cover more ground and see more of the city than you would on foot, while still being eco-friendly and easy to use.

Accommodations

Seville is a popular tourist destination in Spain, attracting millions of visitors each year. As such, the city has a wide range of accommodation options to suit all budgets and preferences. From luxury hotels to budget-friendly hostels and everything in between, there is no shortage of places to stay in Seville.

Hotels

Seville has a fantastic selection of hotels, ranging from budget-friendly options to five-star luxury accommodations. The city's historic center is home to many charming boutique hotels, housed in beautifully restored historic buildings. These hotels offer an authentic Sevillian experience and are often located within walking distance of the city's main attractions.

For travelers seeking more luxury, Seville also has several five-star hotels that offer top-notch amenities such as spa services, rooftop pools, and Michelin-starred restaurants. These hotels are often housed in grand historic buildings, such as palaces and former convents, adding to the charm and character of the city.

Hostels

Seville is also home to many hostels, making it an ideal destination for budget-conscious travelers. These hostels offer dormitory-style accommodations as well as private rooms, making them a great choice for solo travelers, couples, and groups.

Many of the hostels in Seville are located in the city center, making it easy to explore the city's attractions on foot. They also offer a range of amenities such as free Wi-Fi, laundry facilities, and communal kitchens.

Apartments

Another popular option for travelers to Seville is renting an apartment. This is an excellent option for families or larger groups who prefer more space and privacy than a hotel or hostel can offer.

Seville has many apartments for rent, ranging from simple studios to large, luxurious apartments with multiple bedrooms and bathrooms. They often come equipped with kitchens, making it easy to prepare meals and save money on dining out.

Other options

In addition to hotels, hostels, and apartments, Seville has many other unique accommodation options. For example, visitors can stay in historic homes that have been converted into vacation rentals, such as traditional Andalusian houses or former palaces.

There are also several campsites located outside of the city, making it a great option for those who enjoy camping and outdoor activities.

Overall, Seville offers a wide range of accommodation options to suit every budget and preference. Whether you're looking for a luxury hotel or a budget-friendly hostel, there are plenty of options to choose from. To make the most of your trip to Seville, it's important to research and book your accommodation in advance, particularly during peak tourist seasons.

Budget-Friendly Hotels with Luxurious Amenities

You can enjoy a luxurious stay without breaking the bank by choosing from the city's many budget-friendly hotels with luxurious amenities. These hotels offer excellent value for money, with comfortable rooms and facilities that will make guests feel pampered and relaxed.

Hotel Don Paco

Located in the heart of Seville's historic center, Hotel Don Paco is a three-star hotel that offers comfortable rooms at an affordable price. The hotel's rooftop pool is a highlight, with stunning views of the city's skyline and the perfect spot for a refreshing dip on a hot day.

The hotel's rooms are attractively appointed and have comfortable mattresses as well as contemporary facilities such as air conditioning, flat-screen TVs, and complimentary Wi-Fi. The hotel also features a bar and restaurant that serves delectable local food as well as delightful beverages.

Hotel Murillo

Hotel Murillo is a charming two-star hotel located in the heart of Seville's Santa Cruz neighborhood, just a few minutes walk from the city's main attractions such as the Cathedral and the Giralda Tower. The hotel's rooms are cozy and comfortable, with traditional Andalusian décor and modern amenities such as air conditioning, flat-screen TVs, and free Wi-Fi.

The hotel also features a rooftop terrace with beautiful city views, which is a perfect location to unwind and have a drink after a long day of touring. Guests may also use the hotel's bike rental facility to explore the city at their leisure.

Hotel Casa 1800

Hotel Casa 1800 is a four-star boutique hotel located in a restored 19th-century mansion in the heart of Seville's historic center. The hotel's rooms are elegant and spacious, with high ceilings, traditional Andalusian décor, and modern amenities such as air conditioning, flat-screen TVs, and free Wi-Fi.

The hotel's rooftop terrace offers stunning views of the city's skyline, while the courtyard garden is a tranquil oasis in the heart of the bustling city. The hotel also has a spa, offering a range of treatments and massages to help guests unwind and relax.

Hotel Boutique Palacio Pinello

Located in a restored 16th-century palace in the heart of Seville's historic center, Hotel Boutique Palacio Pinello is a stylish four-star hotel that offers a luxurious stay at an affordable price. The hotel's rooms are spacious and elegant, with traditional Andalusian décor and modern amenities such as air conditioning, flat-screen TVs, and free Wi-Fi.

The hotel's rooftop terrace is a highlight, offering stunning views of the city's skyline and the perfect spot for a romantic evening drink. The hotel also has a restaurant serving delicious local cuisine, as well as a bar and lounge area for guests to relax and unwind.

By booking in advance, travelers can find the perfect hotel to suit their needs and budget, ensuring a memorable and enjoyable stay in this beautiful city.

Hostels with a High-End Vibe

When it comes to budget-friendly accommodation in Seville, hostels are often the top choice. However, not all hostels have the same level of quality and comfort. Some hostels in Seville offer more luxurious amenities and a high-end vibe that will make you feel like you're staying in a fancy hotel. Here are some of the best hostels in Seville with a high-end vibe:

The Boutique Hostel: This stylish and modern hostel is located in the heart of Seville, just a few steps from the Cathedral and the Alcazar. The Boutique Hostel features private rooms and dorms with en-suite bathrooms, air conditioning, and free Wi-Fi.

The hostel also has a rooftop terrace with stunning views of the city, a bar, and a lounge area with a flat-screen TV and a pool table.

Oasis Backpackers Hostel: This award-winning hostel is situated in a historic building in the center of Seville, close to many of the city's top attractions. Oasis Backpackers Hostel offers private rooms and dorms with comfortable beds, air conditioning, and free Wi-Fi. The hostel also has a rooftop terrace with a swimming pool, a bar, and a restaurant that serves delicious Andalusian cuisine.

Hostel One Catedral: This cozy and friendly hostel is located in a traditional Andalusian house in the heart of Seville, just a few minutes walk from the Cathedral and the Alcazar. Hostel One Catedral features private rooms and dorms with comfortable beds, air conditioning, and free Wi-Fi. The hostel also offers free breakfast, a communal kitchen, and a rooftop terrace with views of the city.

Black Swan Hostel: This trendy and stylish hostel is located in a historic building in the center of Seville, close to many bars, restaurants, and shops. Black Swan Hostel offers private rooms and dorms with comfortable beds, air conditioning, and free Wi-Fi. The hostel also has a rooftop terrace with a swimming pool, a bar, and a lounge area with a flat-screen TV and a pool table.

La Banda Rooftop Hostel: This modern and stylish hostel is located in the trendy Alameda de Hércules neighborhood, just a short walk from many of Seville's top attractions. La Banda Rooftop Hostel offers private rooms and dorms with comfortable beds, air conditioning, and free Wi-Fi. The hostel also has a rooftop terrace with a swimming pool, a bar, and a lounge area with a flat-screen TV and a pool table.

These hostels in Seville offer much more than just a place to sleep. They provide a high-end vibe with luxurious amenities, friendly staff, and a welcoming atmosphere. They are perfect for travelers who want to experience Seville's vibrant nightlife and cultural attractions while staying in a comfortable and stylish environment.

Affordable Airbnb with a Touch of Luxury

There are many affordable Airbnb with a touch of luxury in Seville, which provide comfortable and stylish accommodations for budget-conscious travelers. These Airbnbs often feature unique decor, high-end amenities, and excellent locations in the heart of Seville's most vibrant neighborhoods.

One of the best neighborhoods to look for an affordable Airbnb with a touch of luxury is the historic Santa Cruz district. This neighborhood is home to some of Seville's most picturesque streets, and many of the Airbnbs in this area feature beautiful balconies, traditional Andalusian architecture, and modern amenities such as air conditioning and free Wi-Fi.

Another popular neighborhood to look for an affordable Airbnb is Triana, located across the Guadalquivir River from the historic city center. Triana is known for its lively atmosphere, traditional ceramic workshops, and excellent tapas bars. Many of the Airbnbs in this area feature beautiful views of the river and the city skyline, as well as stylish decor and modern amenities.

For those looking for a more secluded and quiet experience, the Macarena neighborhood is an excellent option. This area is home to many traditional Sevillian houses and is located just a short walk from some of Seville's most popular attractions, such as the Basilica of La Macarena and the Alameda de Hércules. Many of the Airbnbs in this area feature beautiful outdoor patios and gardens, as well as stylish interiors and comfortable furnishings.

When searching for an affordable Airbnb with a touch of luxury in Seville, it's important to read reviews from previous guests to get an idea of the property's quality and location. Additionally, it's a good idea to communicate with the host and ask any questions you may have before booking, such as the proximity to public transportation, the availability of parking, and the check-in and check-out times.

Whether you're looking for a stylish and centrally located apartment in the heart of Santa Cruz or a cozy and secluded house in the Macarena neighborhood, there's sure to be an Airbnb that fits your budget and preferences

Tips for finding and booking accommodations in Seville

Finding and booking accommodations in Seville can be an overwhelming task, especially if you're unfamiliar with the city or traveling on a budget. However, with a few tips and tricks, you can find the perfect accommodations for your needs and budget.

Determine your budget: Before you start looking for accommodations in Seville, it's essential to determine your budget. Seville offers a wide range of accommodations, from budget-friendly hostels to high-end hotels, so knowing your budget will help you narrow down your search and save time.

Use multiple booking platforms: To find the best deals on accommodations, it's essential to use multiple booking platforms, such as Booking.com, Airbnb, and Expedia. Each platform offers a different selection of accommodations, and prices can vary between them, so it's a good idea to compare prices and read reviews from previous guests.

Research the neighborhoods: Seville is a diverse city with many different neighborhoods, each with its unique character and attractions. Before booking your accommodations, research the neighborhoods to find the best location for your needs. For example, if you're interested in Seville's historic landmarks and attractions, the Santa Cruz neighborhood is an excellent option, while if you're interested in nightlife, the Triana neighborhood is a great choice.

Check the amenities: When booking accommodations in Seville, it's important to check the amenities offered by the property. Depending on your needs, you may want to look for accommodations with air conditioning, free Wi-Fi, a kitchen, or a balcony with a view. Additionally, check if the property offers any extra services, such as airport transfers or breakfast.

Read reviews: Reading reviews from previous guests is a great way to get an idea of the quality of the accommodations and the level of service provided. Look for reviews that mention cleanliness, location, and staff friendliness, as these are essential factors that can greatly impact your stay.

Contact the host: If you have any questions or concerns about the accommodations, it's a good idea to contact the host before booking. The host can provide you with more information about the property and the neighborhood, as well as answer any questions you may have about check-in and check-out times or amenities.

Book early: Seville is a popular tourist destination, especially during peak season, so it's essential to book your accommodations early to secure the best deals and availability. Booking early also gives you more time to plan your trip and ensure everything is in order before your arrival.

With these tips, you can find the perfect accommodations for your needs and budget and enjoy a comfortable and memorable stay in this beautiful city.

Chapter2: What To See and Do in Seville

Top attractions in Seville

Seville is a city that is rich in culture and history, with a variety of attractions that draw visitors from all over the world. Among the top attractions in Seville are the Cathedral, Alcazar, and Plaza de España.

The Cathedral

Seville's Cathedral is one of the city's most iconic landmarks and is considered the largest Gothic cathedral in the world. It was built on the site of a former mosque in the 12th century, and it took over a century to complete the cathedral's construction. Visitors can explore the cathedral's ornate interior, which features intricate carvings, stunning stained glass windows, and a breathtaking altarpiece.

One of the most popular features of the Cathedral is the Giralda Tower, which was originally built as a minaret during the Muslim rule of Spain. Visitors can climb to the top of the tower for spectacular views of the city. The climb to the top is not strenuous, as the tower features ramps instead of stairs. The Giralda Tower is a great place to get panoramic views of Seville, and visitors should try to time their visit for a sunset or sunrise view.

Alcazar

The Alcazar is a palace complex that was built by the Moorish rulers of Spain in the 14th century. The palace is a stunning example of Mudéjar architecture, which is a style that combines Islamic and Christian elements. The palace has been used as a residence for Spanish royalty throughout the centuries and is still used by the Spanish royal family today.

The Alcazar's gardens are a must-see attraction. They feature beautiful courtyards, fountains, and pools, and are perfect for strolling through and enjoying the peaceful atmosphere. The gardens also feature many different types of flora, including fruit trees, cypress trees, and exotic plants.

The palace's interior is just as impressive as its exterior, with intricate tilework, ornate archways, and intricate carvings. The royal apartments are particularly noteworthy, with beautifully decorated ceilings and walls, and ornate furnishings.

Plaza de España

The Plaza de España is a stunning example of neo-Mudéjar architecture, built for the 1929 World's Fair. The plaza features a large central fountain, surrounded by a semicircular building that houses government offices. Visitors can take a boat ride on the canal that runs through the center of the plaza, or simply stroll through the gardens and admire the beautiful tilework.

The Plaza de España is a great place to relax and enjoy the sunshine. The plaza's benches are decorated with ceramic tiles that depict scenes from each of Spain's provinces, making it a popular spot for photos. In the evenings, the plaza is often filled with street performers and musicians, creating a festive atmosphere.

Other Attractions

While the Cathedral, Alcazar, and Plaza de España are Seville's most famous attractions, the city is home to many other noteworthy sites. The Santa Cruz neighborhood, for example, is one of Seville's most charming areas, with narrow streets, flower-filled courtyards, and historic buildings. The neighborhood was once the Jewish quarter of Seville and is now home to some of the city's best tapas bars and restaurants.

The Metropol Parasol is a modern landmark in Seville's old town, designed by the German architect Jürgen Mayer. The structure, which has been dubbed the "mushrooms" by locals, is the largest wooden structure in the world and houses a market, a concert venue, and a rooftop terrace with panoramic views of the city.

The Casa de Pilatos is a Renaissance palace that was built in the 16th century by the Marquis of Tarifa. The palace features a beautiful mix of Mudéjar and Renaissance architecture, with intricate tile work, ornate ceilings, and beautiful gardens. Visitors can explore the palace's many rooms, including the chapel, the courtyard, and the beautiful gardens. The palace also houses a collection of paintings and sculptures, including works by Murillo and Zurbarán.

Another popular attraction in Seville is the Triana neighborhood, which is located across the Guadalquivir River from the city center. Triana is known for its vibrant atmosphere and is home to many artisan workshops, flamenco bars, and traditional restaurants. Visitors can explore the neighborhood's narrow streets and admire the colorful ceramics that are made in the area.

Finally, the Torre del Oro is another of Seville's iconic landmarks. The tower was built in the 13th century as part of the city's defense system and was later used as a prison and as a navigational landmark for ships entering the city's port. Today, the tower houses a maritime museum, where visitors can learn about Seville's maritime history.

You are sure to be captivated by its charm and beauty, and likely to leave with memories that will last a lifetime.

Recommendations for exploring Seville's neighborhoods and historical landmarks

Seville is a city that is rich in history and culture, and exploring its many neighborhoods and historical landmarks is a great way to get a sense of its unique charm and character. Here are some recommendations for exploring Seville's neighborhoods and historical landmarks:

Take a Walking Tour

One of the best ways to explore Seville's neighborhoods and historical landmarks is by taking a walking tour. Many tour companies offer guided tours that will take you through the city's most iconic neighborhoods and landmarks, allowing you to learn about the history and culture of the city. Walking tours are a great way to get oriented in a new city, and they can help you to discover hidden gems and off-the-beaten-path attractions that you might not have found on your own.

Explore the Santa Cruz Neighborhood

The Santa Cruz neighborhood is one of Seville's most charming and picturesque areas, with narrow cobblestone streets, white-washed buildings, and colorful flower-filled balconies. This neighborhood was once home to Seville's Jewish community, and today it is known for its lively atmosphere, its many tapas bars and restaurants, and its many shops and boutiques. Be sure to visit the Plaza de Santa Cruz, which is surrounded by orange trees and is home to a beautiful church and a lovely fountain.

Visit the Cathedral and Giralda Tower

The Cathedral of Seville is one of the city's most iconic landmarks, and it is a must-visit attraction for anyone traveling to the city. The Cathedral is the biggest Gothic cathedral in the world, and it has the tomb of Christopher Columbus. Be sure to climb the

Giralda Tower, which offers stunning views of the city.

Explore the Alcazar

The Alcazar is another of Seville's iconic landmarks, and it is a beautiful example of Mudéjar architecture. The palace was built in the 14th century for King Peter of Castile, and it is now a UNESCO World Heritage Site. Visitors can explore the palace's many rooms, including the beautiful gardens, the Courtyard of the Maidens, and the Hall of Ambassadors.

Visit the Plaza de España

The Plaza de España is one of Seville's most famous landmarks, and it is a beautiful example of Spanish Renaissance architecture. The plaza was built in 1929 for the Ibero-American Exposition, and it is now a popular tourist attraction. Visitors can take a stroll around the plaza, admire the colorful tiled alcoves that represent each province of Spain, and take a boat ride in the moat.

Take a Horse Carriage Ride

Taking a horse carriage ride through Seville's streets is a romantic and charming way to explore the city. Carriage drivers can often be found near major tourist attractions, and they will take you on a scenic tour of the city's most beautiful landmarks and neighborhoods. Horse carriage rides are especially popular at night when the city is illuminated and the streets are less crowded.

Rent a Bike or Scooter

Renting a bike or scooter is a great way to explore Seville's neighborhoods and landmarks at your own pace. There are many bike and scooter rental shops located throughout the city, and most offer daily or hourly rentals. Biking or scootering through Seville's streets can be a fun and exciting way to discover the city's hidden gems and off-the-beaten-path attractions.

Overall, exploring Seville's neighborhoods and historical landmarks is a great way to get a sense of the city's unique charm and character. Whether you take a walking tour, visit the Cathedral and Alcazar, or simply wander through the city's charming streets and alleys, you are sure to be captivated by Seville's beauty and charm.

Information on museums, galleries, and other cultural institutions in Seville

Seville is a city rich in culture and history, and there are many museums, galleries, and other cultural institutions that are worth visiting. Here are some of the top cultural institutions to explore in Seville:

Museum of Fine Arts

The Museum of Fine Arts is one of Seville's most valuable art museums, and it features a large collection of works by some of Spain's most important artists. The museum is housed in a former convent, and it features paintings, sculptures, and other works of art from the Middle Ages to the present day.

Archaeological Museum

The Archaeological Museum is another of Seville's most important museums, and it features an extensive collection of archaeological artifacts from prehistoric times to the Roman Empire. The museum is located in the historic center of Seville, and it is housed in a former palace that was built in the 16th century.

Flamenco Dance Museum

The Flamenco Dance Museum is a unique museum that is dedicated to the art of flamenco dance. The museum features exhibits on the history and culture of flamenco, as well as live flamenco performances by some of the best dancers in Spain.

Contemporary Art Museum

The Contemporary Art Museum is a modern art museum that features works by some of the most important contemporary artists in Spain and around the world. The museum is located in a former monastery, and it features a wide range of contemporary art, including paintings, sculptures, installations, and video art.

Palace of the Countess of Lebrija

The Palace of the Countess of Lebrija is a beautiful palace that features an extensive collection of Roman mosaics. The palace was built in the 16th century, and it is one of Seville's most important historic buildings. The mosaics at the palace are some of the best preserved in Spain, and they offer a fascinating glimpse into the lives of the Romans who once lived in Seville.

Bullfighting Museum

The Bullfighting Museum is a unique museum that is dedicated to the art and culture of bullfighting. The museum features exhibits on the history and traditions of bullfighting, as well as artifacts and memorabilia from some of Spain's most famous bullfighters.

Casa de la Memoria

Casa de la Memoria is a cultural institution that is dedicated to preserving and promoting the art of flamenco music. The institution hosts live flamenco performances by some of the best musicians in Spain, and it is a great place to experience the passion and energy of this unique musical form.

Seville is a city that is rich in culture and history, and there are many museums, galleries, and other cultural institutions that are worth exploring. Whether you are interested in art, archaeology, flamenco dance, or bullfighting, there is something for everyone in Seville's vibrant cultural scene.

Free and Low-Cost Activities

Seville has many affordable and enjoyable activities to offer. From playing sports in the park to taking a flamenco dance class or visiting the Archaeological Museum, there is something for everyone. Here are some free and low-cost activities to do in Seville:

Explore the Parks

Seville has many beautiful parks that are free to visit, including Maria Luisa Park, Alamillo Park, and the Gardens of the Murillo. These parks are great places to relax and enjoy the city's natural beauty, and they are also popular spots for picnics and outdoor activities.

Visit the City's Churches

Seville is known for its beautiful churches, and many of them are free to visit. Some of the most popular churches to visit include the Church of El Salvador, the Church of San Luis de los Franceses, and the Church of Santa Maria la Blanca.

Walk Along the River

The Guadalquivir River runs through Seville, and it is a beautiful spot for a leisurely walk. The river offers great views of the city's skyline and the surrounding countryside, and there are many bars and restaurants along the riverfront where you can stop for a drink or a snack.

Visit the Markets

Seville has several markets that are worth visiting, including the Triana Market and the Encarnación Market. These markets offer a wide range of goods, from fresh produce to local crafts, and they are great places to soak up the city's vibrant atmosphere.

Enjoy the Street Art

Seville is home to many talented street artists, and there are several areas of the city where you can see their work. Some of the best places to find street art in Seville include the Alameda de Hércules and the Macarena neighborhood.

Take a Free Walking Tour

Several companies in Seville offer free walking tours of the city, including Sandeman's New Europe Tours and Free Walking Tour Seville. These tours are a great way to learn about the city's history and culture, and they are a budget-friendly way to see the sights.

Visit the University of Seville

The University of Seville is one of the oldest universities in Spain, and it is home to several beautiful historic buildings. Visitors can tour the university's campuses and see its historic buildings, including the Old Tobacco Factory, which was the inspiration for Bizet's opera Carmen.

Rent a Bike

Seville is a bike-friendly city, with many bike lanes and paths. Renting a bike is a great way to explore the city at your own pace and get some exercise at the same time. Several bike rental companies offer affordable rates, and there are also guided bike tours available for those who want to learn more about the city's history and culture.

Play Sports in the Park

Seville has many parks with facilities for sports like soccer, basketball, and tennis. These facilities are free to use, and you can often find locals playing pick-up games. Bring a ball or racket and join in on the fun.

Go for a Run

If you enjoy running, Seville has many great routes to explore. You can run along the river, through the parks, or around the city's historic center. The city also hosts several running events throughout the year, including the Seville Marathon and the Nocturnal Race.

Take a Flamenco Dance Class

Flamenco is an integral part of Seville's culture, and taking a flamenco dance class is a fun way to learn about this art form. There are many dance schools and studios in Seville that offer classes for all levels, and some even offer free trial classes.

Attend a Local Festival

Seville is known for its many festivals, and attending one is a great way to experience the city's culture and traditions. Some of the most popular festivals include the April Fair, the Corpus Christi

Festival, and the Christmas Fair. Many of these festivals are free to attend, and they offer a unique glimpse into Seville's customs and traditions.

Visit the Archaeological Museum

The Archaeological Museum of Seville is a great place to learn about the history of the city and the surrounding region. The museum's collection includes artifacts from prehistoric times to the Roman Empire, and it offers a fascinating look into Seville's past. Entry to the museum is free on Tuesdays.

Take a Day Trip

Seville is surrounded by many beautiful towns and villages that are worth visiting. Take a day trip to nearby destinations like Carmona, Osuna, or Écija to explore their historic landmarks, sample local cuisine, and enjoy the scenery.

Don't forget to take advantage of the city's many festivals and nearby day trip opportunities as well.

Day Trips from Seville

Seville is a great home base for exploring nearby destinations that offer a glimpse into Andalusian culture and history. Here are some suggestions for nearby destinations to visit:

Cordoba

Located about 1.5 hours from Seville by train, Cordoba is a must-visit destination for those interested in history, architecture, and culture. The city's star attraction is the Mezquita, a stunning mosque-cathedral that dates back to the 8th century. Other highlights include the Alcazar de los Reyes Cristianos, a 14th-century palace and fortress, and the Jewish Quarter, which features narrow streets lined with whitewashed houses.

Granada

Home to the famous Alhambra Palace, Granada is a city steeped in history and culture. The Alhambra is a 14th-century palace and fortress complex that features intricate Islamic architecture and beautiful gardens. Other highlights of Granada include the historic Albaicin neighborhood, the flamenco scene, and the vibrant street life.

Ronda

Perched on a cliff overlooking a dramatic gorge, Ronda is one of the most picturesque towns in Andalusia. The town's star attraction is the Puente Nuevo, an 18th-century bridge that spans the gorge and offers stunning views. Other highlights of Ronda include the old town, which features narrow streets and historic buildings, and the Plaza de Toros, one of Spain's oldest bullfighting rings.

Jerez de la Frontera

Located about an hour south of Seville, Jerez de la Frontera is a charming town known for its sherry and flamenco. Visitors can tour the many sherry bodegas in town, including the famous Tio Pepe bodega, or take in a flamenco show at one of the town's many venues.

Cadiz

Located on the Atlantic coast, Cadiz is a historic port city known for its seafood, beaches, and charming old town. Highlights of Cadiz include the 18th-century cathedral, the Torre Tavira, a historic watchtower with panoramic views of the city, and the Central Market, where visitors can sample the local seafood.

These nearby destinations are all easily accessible from Seville and offer a great way to experience more of Andalusia's rich history and culture.

Transportation options and timing for day trips from Seville

Cordoba

Cordoba is about 1.5 hours away from Seville by train. Trains depart from Seville's Santa Justa station, and there are several departures throughout the day. The last train from Cordoba to Seville departs around 9:30 pm, so it's possible to spend a full day in Cordoba and return to Seville in the evening.

Granada

Granada is about 2.5 hours away from Seville by bus or train. Buses depart from Seville's Plaza de Armas station, while trains depart from Santa Justa station. There are several departures throughout the day for both options. It's recommended to leave early in the morning to make the most of the day trip and plan to return to Seville in the evening.

Ronda

Ronda is about 1.5 hours away from Seville by bus or train. Buses depart from Seville's Plaza de Armas station, while trains depart from Santa Justa station. There are several departures throughout the day for both options. It's recommended to leave in the morning and return to Seville in the evening.

Jerez de la Frontera

Jerez de la Frontera is about 1 hour away from Seville by train. Trains depart from Santa Justa station, and there are several departures throughout the day. It's possible to spend a full day in Jerez and return to Seville in the evening.

Cadiz

Cadiz is about 1.5 hours away from Seville by train. Trains depart from Santa Justa station, and there are several departures throughout the day. It's possible to spend a full day in Cadiz and return to Seville in the evening.

It's recommended to book train or bus tickets in advance to ensure availability and to save time at the station. It's also a good idea to plan out your day trip in advance and consider any specific attractions or activities you'd like to visit while there. With a little planning, day trips from Seville can be a great way to explore more of Andalusia's rich culture and history.

Tips for planning a day trip from Seville

Planning a day trip from Seville can be an exciting way to explore nearby destinations in Andalusia. Here are some tips to help you plan a successful day trip:

1. Choose your destination wisely: Take into consideration the distance and travel time to your desired destination. It's recommended to choose a destination that is no more than 2-3

hours away from Seville. This will give you enough time to explore the area without feeling rushed.

2. Research transportation options: Look up the different transportation options available for your chosen destination. This can include trains, buses, and private tours. Check schedules, ticket prices, and travel time to find the best option that fits your schedule and budget.

3. Plan your itinerary: Before leaving for your day trip, plan out your itinerary for the day. Research the top attractions and activities to do in the area and prioritize which ones you'd like to visit. Make sure to consider any entrance fees, opening and closing times, and how much time you need to explore each attraction.

4. Pack essentials: Bring along any essential items you may need for your day trips, such

as sunscreen, water, snacks, and comfortable shoes. It's also a good idea to bring a map or guidebook of the area to help you navigate.

5. Leave early: To make the most of your day trip, it's recommended to leave early in the morning. This will give you plenty of time to explore the area and return to Seville in the evening.

6. Be flexible: While it's important to have a plan, it's also important to be flexible. Unexpected delays or changes in plans can happen, so be prepared to adjust your itinerary if needed.

By following these tips, you can plan a successful day trip from Seville and make the most of your time in Andalusia.

Chapter3: Dinning, Nightlife And Entertainment in Seville

Seville's culinary scene

Seville's culinary scene is a vibrant and diverse one, with a range of traditional dishes and drinks that showcase the city's rich history and cultural heritage. From hearty stews to sweet pastries, Seville has something for everyone when it comes to food and drink.

One of the most iconic dishes in Seville is the Andalusian gazpacho, a cold soup made with tomatoes, peppers, cucumber, and garlic. It is typically served as a refreshing appetizer on hot summer days. Another popular dish is the salmorejo, a thicker version of gazpacho made with bread crumbs, garlic, and olive oil. It is often topped with diced jamón serrano, boiled eggs, and croutons.

Another must-try dish in Seville is the rabo de toro, a hearty oxtail stew cooked in red wine and spices. It is typically served with potatoes or rice and is a favorite among locals and visitors alike. Other traditional meat dishes include the secreto ibérico, a grilled pork dish, and the cabrilla, a slow-cooked beef cheek in red wine.

Seafood lovers should try the fritura mixta, a fried seafood platter that includes a variety of fish and shellfish such as squid, prawns, and white bait. The pescaíto frito, a similar dish featuring smaller fish such as anchovies and sardines, is also a popular option. For those who prefer something lighter, the espinacas con garbanzos is a vegetarian dish made with spinach and chickpeas that is both nutritious and flavorful.

In addition to the savory dishes, Seville is also known for its sweet treats. One of the most popular is the pestiños, a honey-soaked pastry made with flour, olive oil, and anise. Another local favorite is the torrijas, a type of French toast soaked in milk and flavored with cinnamon and sugar.

No culinary journey in Seville would be complete without trying some of the city's famous drinks. One of the most popular is the tinto de verano, a refreshing summer drink made with red wine and lemon soda. The rebujito, a mix of fino sherry and lemon soda, is another popular choice, particularly during the annual Feria de Abril festival. And of course, no trip to Seville would be complete without trying the local sherry, which comes in a variety of styles including fino, manzanilla, and oloroso.

Seville's culinary scene is diverse and caters to all tastes and budgets. Visitors can find traditional tapas bars serving small plates of local specialties, as well as upscale restaurants offering modern interpretations of classic dishes. The city also has a growing number of vegetarian and vegan options, as well as international cuisines such as sushi and Mexican food.

Seville's culinary scene is a must-see for any food lover visiting the city. From traditional dishes to modern interpretations, Seville has something to offer everyone. Be sure to sample some of the city's iconic dishes and drinks to get a true taste of Andalusia's rich cultural heritage.

Budget-friendly restaurants and bars, as well as high-end dining experiences

Seville is a city that offers a wide range of dining options, from traditional tapas bars to high-end Michelin-starred restaurants. Whether you're looking for a budget-friendly meal or a luxurious dining experience, there's something for everyone in Seville.

For budget-friendly options, Seville has plenty of tapas bars, and restaurants that offer traditional Spanish dishes at affordable prices. One popular option is La Bodega, a traditional tapas bar located in the historic center of the city. Here you can try a variety of dishes, including tortilla de patatas (Spanish omelette), croquetas (croquettes), and chorizo al vino (chorizo in wine sauce), all at very reasonable prices.

Another popular budget-friendly option is El Rinconcillo, one of the oldest bars in Seville. Here you can enjoy traditional tapas dishes in a historic setting, with prices that won't break the bank. Don't miss the spinach and chickpeas dish, a local specialty.

For a more upscale dining experience, Seville also has plenty of high-end restaurants to choose from.

One of the most famous is Abantal, which has been awarded a Michelin star for its innovative cuisine. The menu features creative dishes that blend traditional Andalusian ingredients with modern techniques.

Another high-end option is Eslava, which is known for its innovative take on traditional Spanish dishes. The restaurant has a modern and stylish atmosphere, and the menu features dishes like slow-cooked Iberian pork and grilled octopus.

If you're looking for a luxurious dining experience with a view, head to the rooftop restaurant at the EME Catedral Hotel. The restaurant offers panoramic views of the city and serves a range of dishes, from traditional Spanish cuisine to sushi.

In addition to these options, Seville has plenty of other restaurants and bars to explore. For a more authentic experience, try visiting a local Mercado (market) where you can sample a variety of fresh and local ingredients. Mercado Lonja del Barranco and Mercado de Triana are both popular options for foodies.

When it comes to drinks, Seville is famous for its sherry wine. The city has a long tradition of sherry production, and you can find a wide range of varieties to try in local bars and restaurants. For a true taste of Seville, try a glass of manzanilla, a light, and dry sherry that pairs well with seafood.

Seville is also known for its local beer, Cruzcampo. You can find this refreshing beer in bars and restaurants throughout the city. For a more unique drinking experience, try visiting a local vermutería, a bar that specializes in vermouth. Vermouth is a fortified wine that's often served with a variety of tapas dishes.

Seville's culinary scene offers something for everyone, from budget-friendly tapas bars to high-end Michelin-starred restaurants. Whether you're looking to sample traditional Spanish dishes or innovative cuisine, you're sure to find something to satisfy your taste buds in this vibrant city.

Tips for navigating Seville's tapas culture

Tapas are perfect for sharing with friends and family, allowing you to sample a range of different flavors and textures. However, for first-time visitors to Seville, the tapas scene can seem overwhelming and confusing.

Here are some tips for navigating Seville's tapas culture and making the most of your culinary experience.

Know the etiquette

Tapas in Seville are meant to be shared, so it's important to know the etiquette before you dive in. If you're in a group, order a variety of different dishes to share and take turns choosing what to order. It's also common to order a drink with your tapas, such as a glass of wine or a beer. When you're finished, simply let the bartender know how many tapas you've had and they will add it to your bill.

Try a variety of dishes

One of the best things about tapas is the variety of dishes available. Don't be afraid to try new things and order dishes that you wouldn't normally choose. Some popular tapas dishes in Seville include tortilla de Camarones (shrimp omelet), salmorejo (a cold tomato soup), and cabrilla (braised pork cheeks). Don't forget to also try the local cheeses and cured meats, such as jamón ibérico.

Head off the beaten path

While there are plenty of great tapas bars in the tourist areas of Seville, some of the best and most authentic tapas experiences can be found off the beaten path. Explore the side streets and neighborhoods of Seville to find hidden gems and local favorites. You can also ask locals for recommendations, as they often have insider knowledge of the best tapas bars in the city.

Look for specials and deals

Many tapas bars in Seville offer daily specials or deals, such as a free tapa with a drink or a discount for ordering multiple dishes. Look out for chalkboards or signs advertising these deals, or simply ask the bartender what the specials of the day are. This can be a great way to try new dishes without breaking the bank.

Go on a tapas tour

If you're feeling overwhelmed by the abundance of tapas options in Seville, consider going on a tapas tour. These guided tours will take you to some of the best tapas bars in the city, where you can sample a range of different dishes and learn about the history and culture of tapas in Seville. This is also a great way to meet other travelers and make new friends.

Time your tapas crawl

In Seville, the traditional time for tapas is in the evening, usually between 8 pm and 11 pm. This is when the bars and restaurants are at their busiest and the atmosphere is at its liveliest. However, if you're on a budget, consider going for lunch instead. Many tapas bars in Seville offer a fixed-price lunch menu, which can be a great way to try a variety of dishes at a more affordable price

Don't forget the drinks

While tapas are the star of the show in Seville, don't forget to also sample the local drinks. Sherry is a popular choice, particularly the sweet Pedro

Ximénez variety. You can also try a rebujito, a refreshing cocktail made with sherry and lemonade, or a tinto de verano, a chilled red wine with soda water.

Seville's tapas culture is a must-try experience for any traveler visiting the city. With these tips in mind, you can navigate the tapas scene with ease.

Seville's nightlife scene

Seville is known for its vibrant nightlife scene, offering a variety of options for those looking to enjoy a night out. Here's an overview of Seville's nightlife scene:

Bars: Seville has a wide range of bars, from traditional tapas bars to modern cocktail bars. Many bars offer outdoor seating, making it a great place to enjoy a drink and people-watch. Some popular areas for bars include Alameda de Hércules and Calle

Betis, which offer a variety of options to choose from.

Clubs: Seville has several nightclubs that cater to a variety of music tastes. Some popular clubs include Sala X and Antique Theatre, which host both local and international DJs. Clubs usually don't get busy until after midnight, and it's not uncommon for them to stay open until 6 or 7 am.

Flamenco Shows: Flamenco is a traditional dance form that originated in Andalusia, and Seville is one of the best places to experience it. Several venues in Seville offer flamenco shows, ranging from traditional performances in small intimate settings to large productions in theaters. Some popular venues include Casa de la Memoria and La Carbonería.

Rooftop Bars: Seville is home to several rooftop bars that offer stunning views of the city skyline. Many of these bars are located on the rooftops of hotels, such as EME Catedral Hotel and Hotel Doña Maria. These bars are perfect for enjoying a drink and watching the sunset over the city.

Pub Crawls: For those looking to explore Seville's nightlife scene with a group, pub crawls are a popular option. Several companies offer pub crawls, which typically include visiting several bars and clubs in one night. This is a great way to meet other travelers and · locals and experience Seville's nightlife scene.

Seville's nightlife is a great way to experience the city's vibrant culture and socialize with locals and other travelers.

Recommendations for experiencing Seville's nightlife on a budget

Seville's nightlife can be expensive, but there are ways to experience it on a budget. Here are some recommendations for enjoying Seville's nightlife without breaking the bank:

Choose budget-friendly bars: There are plenty of budget-friendly bars in Seville that offer cheap drinks and a great atmosphere. Some popular options include Bar Alfalfa, Bodega Santa Cruz, and Bar El Comercio. These bars offer traditional tapas and drinks at reasonable prices.

Visit during happy hour: Many bars and clubs in Seville offer happy hour specials, usually from around 8 pm to 10 pm. This is a great time to enjoy discounted drinks and snacks before the night gets busy.

Attend free flamenco shows: While some flamenco shows can be expensive, there are free options available as well. For example, La Carbonería offers free flamenco shows every night, and many bars and restaurants also offer free performances during dinner.

Join a free walking tour: Some companies offer free walking tours of Seville's nightlife scene, which can be a great way to explore the city and meet other travelers. These tours often include visits to different bars and clubs, as well as historical and cultural information about the city.

Take advantage of pub crawls: While pub crawls can be expensive, they often include discounts at the bars and clubs they visit, making them a more budget-friendly option. Some companies even offer free pub crawls, where you only pay for your drinks.

Enjoy the outdoors: Seville's warm climate makes it a great place to enjoy the outdoors at night. Many parks and plazas are open late and offer a lively atmosphere, such as Alameda de Hércules and Plaza de España. You can also bring your drinks and snacks to enjoy a picnic in the park.

By using these tips, you can experience the city's vibrant nightlife without spending too much money.

Dress codes and etiquette for Seville's nightlife venues

When it comes to dress codes and etiquette for Seville's nightlife venues, it's important to keep in mind that the city has a strong cultural heritage, and many of its bars and clubs have a dress code and certain etiquette that is expected of visitors.

Dress appropriately: While not all venues have a strict dress code, it's generally a good idea to dress nicely when going out at night in Seville. For men, this may mean wearing slacks or dress pants and a collared shirt, while women may want to wear dress or dressy pants and a blouse.

Avoid showing too much skin: Seville is a conservative city, and it's generally best to avoid clothing that is too revealing, such as shorts or short skirts, particularly if you plan to visit a more upscale venue.

Show respect for cultural traditions: When visiting flamenco shows or other cultural events, it's important to show respect for the performers and the tradition by dressing appropriately and refraining from using your phone during the performance.

Practice good manners: Whether you're at a bar, club, or other nightlife venue, it's important to practice good manners and respect the other patrons. This means avoiding loud or disruptive behavior and being courteous to others.

Follow the rules: Many nightlife venues in Seville have rules and regulations that are designed to keep patrons safe and ensure a good experience for everyone. This may include no smoking, no outside drinks or food, or a dress code. Be sure to follow these rules to avoid any problems or misunderstandings.

Chapter 4: Shopping in Seville

Seville's shopping scene

Seville is a city that is rich in history, culture, and charm, and its shopping scene is no exception. From traditional markets to modern boutiques, Seville offers a variety of shopping options for visitors. Here is an overview of Seville's shopping scene, including some of the best markets and boutiques to explore during your visit.

Markets:

One of the best ways to experience Seville's shopping scene is by exploring its many markets. The city's most famous market is the Mercado de Triana, which is located in the Triana neighborhood. Here, you can find a wide variety of fresh produce, meats, fish, and other local specialties. The market is open daily and is a great place to pick up ingredients for a picnic or to prepare your own meals.

Another popular market in Seville is the Mercado de la Encarnación, also known as the Metropol Parasol. This market is located in the center of the city and is housed under a large, modern structure. Here, you can find a variety of local and international products, including fresh fruits and vegetables, meats, fish, spices, and more.

If you're looking for a more traditional shopping experience, head to the Plaza de la Alfalfa, where you can find a street market selling everything from clothing and accessories to handicrafts and souvenirs. This market is open on weekends and is a great place to find unique items to take home with you.

Boutiques

In addition to its markets, Seville also has a variety of boutiques and specialty stores that offer unique products and experiences. One of the most famous is the Casa de la Guitarra, a store located in the Santa Cruz neighborhood that sells traditional Spanish guitars and offers concerts and classes for visitors.

If you're looking for high-end fashion and accessories, head to the Sierpes and Tetuán streets, which are home to many of the city's top designer boutiques. Here, you can find everything from high-end clothing and accessories to jewelry and other luxury items.

For a more bohemian shopping experience, head to the Alameda de Hércules, a lively square that is home to a variety of vintage and second-hand stores, as well as local designers and artists. Here, you can find unique clothing, accessories, and artwork that reflect Seville's vibrant creative scene.

Tips for Shopping in Seville: No matter where you decide to shop in Seville, there are a few tips that can help make your experience more enjoyable. First, be sure to wear comfortable shoes, as many of the city's streets and markets are cobblestoned and can be uneven. Second, be prepared to haggle, especially in the markets, where vendors may be willing to negotiate on price. Finally, take your time and enjoy the experience – Seville's shopping scene is as much about the atmosphere and the people as it is about the products themselves.

Recommendations for souvenirs and gifts to bring back from Seville

Seville is a city filled with rich culture, history, and stunning architecture, which makes it an excellent destination for souvenir shopping. Whether you're looking for traditional handicrafts, stylish fashion, or unique keepsakes, Seville has a lot to offer.

Handicrafts: Seville is famous for its beautiful and intricate ceramic and pottery work. You can find a wide variety of handcrafted ceramics, from small decorative tiles to large vases and pitchers. Many of these pieces are adorned with traditional Andalusian motifs and patterns, making them a great way to bring a piece of Seville's rich culture back home with you.

Flamenco dresses: If you want to take home a unique piece of Seville's culture, a flamenco dress is an excellent option. These traditional dresses are colorful and vibrant, and they are often adorned with intricate embroidery and lacework. You can find them in a range of styles and prices, from affordable options to high-end designer dresses.

Olive oil: Spain is known for its high-quality olive oil, and Seville is no exception. If you're a foodie or love to cook, consider picking up a bottle of locally produced-olive oil. You can find it at specialty food shops, markets, and even some souvenir shops. It's an excellent way to bring home a taste of Seville's culinary scene.

Fans: Seville is known for its hot and humid summers, which make fans a practical and fashionable accessory. You can find a wide variety of fans in Seville, from cheap paper ones to high-quality hand-painted fans. They come in a range of colors and styles, so you're sure to find one that suits your taste.

Flamenco music: If you're a music lover, consider picking up some Flamenco CDs or vinyl records. Flamenco is an integral part of Seville's culture, and you can find a range of music from traditional to contemporary. Look for local record shops or markets to find the best selection.

Spanish wine: Spain is known for its excellent wines, and Seville is no exception. Look for local wines from the Andalusia region, such as sherry or Rioja. You can find them at specialty wine shops or even some souvenir shops.

Spanish ham: If you're a meat lover, consider picking up some Spanish ham, also known as jamón ibérico. This cured ham is a delicacy in Spain and can be found at specialty food shops and markets. It's a bit pricey, but the taste is unforgettable.

Traditional sweets: Seville is known for its delicious traditional sweets, such as pestiños, torrijas, and mantecados. These are often sold in small bakeries and pastry shops throughout the city. They make an excellent gift for anyone with a sweet tooth.

Whether you're looking for traditional handicrafts or trendy fashion, you're sure to find something that suits your taste and budget.

Tips for bargaining and negotiating prices

Bargaining and negotiating prices can be a fun and exciting part of the shopping experience in Seville.

1. Do Your Research Before hitting the markets, do some research on the items you are interested in buying. Check the prices of similar items at different stores, and get an idea of the general market price for the product. This will help you to identify good deals and know when a price is too high.

2. Start Low When bargaining, always start with a low price. The vendor will often counter with a higher price, and the negotiation can go back and forth until an

agreement is reached. It is important to remember that bargaining is part of the culture in Seville, so don't be afraid to negotiate.

3. Be Polite and Respectful While bargaining, it is important to remain polite and respectful. Avoid being aggressive or rude, as this can quickly end the negotiation. A smile and friendly behavior can go a long way in getting a good deal.

4. Consider Buying Multiple Items If you are interested in buying multiple items from a vendor, consider bargaining for a bulk discount. Many vendors will be willing to offer a discount for multiple purchases.

5. Walk Away if Necessary If you cannot agree on a price, do not be afraid to walk away. Sometimes, vendors will call you back and offer a lower price. Other times, you may

find the same item at another market for a better price.

6. Keep in Mind Quality While bargaining, keep in mind the quality of the item you are interested in buying. A lower price may seem like a good deal, but if the quality is poor, it may not be worth it. Make sure to inspect the item carefully before agreeing on a price.

7. Enjoy the Process Bargaining can be a fun and exciting part of the shopping experience in Seville. Enjoy the process, talk to the vendors, and immerse yourself in the local culture.

By following these tips, you can negotiate with confidence and bring home unique and meaningful items from your trip.

Chapter 5: Practical and Essential Information

Entry requirements

To enter Spain, you will need to provide numerous papers. The prerequisites are as follows:

Passport or national ID card: If you are an EU citizen, you may enter Spain with a valid national ID card. You will need a valid passport if you are not an EU citizen. Your passport or identification card must be valid for the length of your stay in Spain.

Visa: You may require a visa to enter Spain, depending on your nationality and the duration of your stay. Some countries' citizens, such as those from the United States, Canada, Australia, and New Zealand, do not require a visa for stays of up to 90 days within 180 days. Citizens of other nations, on the other hand, may need a visa or resident permission. Specific visa requirements should be confirmed with your country's embassy or consulate in Spain.

Health control form: All visitors to Spain, regardless of country, must fill out a health control form before arriving. This form requests basic personal information, travel data, and COVID-19-related health information. You may fill out the form online before your travel and produce confirmation of completion when you arrive in Spain.

COVID-19 requirements: Travelers visiting Spain may be required to submit evidence of COVID-19 vaccination, a negative PCR test result obtained within 72 hours of arrival, or a negative antigen test result obtained within 48 hours of arrival. However, the requirements can change quickly, so make sure you have the most up-to-date information before your trip.

Travel insurance: Although it is not required by law, having travel insurance that covers unforeseen changes or interruptions during your vacation, such as trip cancellations, medical crises, or lost or stolen baggage, is usually a smart option.

It's crucial to remember that entrance criteria may change fast, so make sure you're up to speed on the most recent information before arranging your trip to Seville. Furthermore, having a backup plan in case of unexpected changes or disruptions during your trip is always a good idea.

itinerary to help

Here's a sample itinerary for a 5-day trip to Seville: Day 1:

- Visit the Seville Cathedral, a UNESCO World Heritage Site and one of the world's largest Gothic cathedrals.
- Climb to the top of the Giralda Tower for sweeping city views.
- Explore the Real Alcázar de Sevilla, a stunning palace and gardens that have been used as a filming location for Game of Thrones.

Day 2:

- Visit the Plaza de España, a grand public square with a beautiful fountain and colorful tiles representing each province of Spain.
- Take a stroll through the charming Santa Cruz neighborhood, with its narrow streets, white-washed houses, and flower-filled balconies.
- In the evening, see a classic flamenco performance.

Day 3:

- Take a day trip to Cordoba to visit the famous Mosque-Cathedral and explore the historic Jewish quarter.
- Stop by the beautiful Medina Azahara, an ancient palace city dating back to the 10th century.

Day 4:

- Visit the Metropol Parasol, a modern architectural wonder that offers stunning views of the city from its rooftop.
- Explore the Triana neighborhood across the Guadalquivir River, known for its vibrant nightlife, traditional ceramic workshops, and tasty tapas bars.
- Take a sunset riverboat ride.

Day 5:

- Visit the Museum of Fine Arts, with a collection of over 16,000 paintings and sculptures from the 15th to the 20th century.

- Take a bike tour through the city's parks and gardens, such as Maria Luisa Park and Alamillo Park.
- Enjoy a farewell dinner at one of the city's many delicious seafood restaurants.

Of course, this is just a sample itinerary, and you can customize it based on your interests and travel style. There are plenty of other attractions, museums, and neighborhoods to explore in Seville, and the city's proximity to other historic cities in Andalusia makes it a great base for day trips.

Language and Cultural Antiques

Important Phrases to Know for Communicating in Seville

While planning to travel to Seville, it's helpful to know some basic phrases in Spanish to communicate with locals. Even if you don't speak the language fluently, making an effort to communicate in Spanish can go a long way in building rapport and making connections with people. Here are some important phrases to know for communicating in Seville:

1. Hola - Hello
2. Buenos días - Good morning
3. Buenas tardes - Good afternoon
4. Buenas noches - Good evening/night
5. Adiós - Goodbye
6. Por favor - Please
7. Gracias - Thank you
8. De nada - You're welcome
9. ¿Habla inglés? - Do you speak English?
10. No entiendo - I don't understand
11. ¿Dónde está...? - Where is...?
12. La cuenta, por favor - Bill, please
13. ¿Cuánto cuesta? - How much does it cost?
14. ¿Puede ayudarme? - Can you help me?
15. Lo siento - I'm sorry

In addition to these phrases, it's helpful to know basic numbers and how to ask for directions. It's also important to keep in mind that while many people in Seville speak English, not everyone does. Making an effort to communicate in Spanish, even if it's just basic phrases, can be greatly appreciated and can make your trip more enjoyable.

Where to Find the Best Cultural Antiques in Seville

For those interested in finding unique cultural artifacts and antiques, Seville has plenty of options to offer.

One of the best places to start is the Calle Feria flea market. This market is held every Thursday and Sunday and is the perfect place to find vintage and antique items. From furniture to jewelry, books to vinyl records, the Calle Feria market has it all. It's a great place to spend a few hours browsing and bargaining with vendors.

For those looking for more high-end antiques, the El Jueves market is a great option. Held every Thursday in the historic Plaza del Cabildo, El Jueves is the oldest flea market in Seville. Here, you can find antique furniture, rare books, vintage clothing, and more. It's important to keep in mind that prices here may be higher than at other markets, so be prepared to negotiate.

If you're interested in antique ceramics, a visit to Cerámica Santa Ana is a must. This ceramics shop has been in operation since 1929 and is known for its beautiful and unique pieces. From plates to vases to decorative tiles, Cerámica Santa Ana has something for everyone.

Another great option for antique shopping in Seville is the Alameda Antiques Market. Held on the first Saturday of every month in the Alameda de Hércules square, this market is a hub for antique lovers. Here, you can find everything from vintage clothing to rare coins to antique furniture. It's a great place to find unique souvenirs or gifts for loved ones back home.

Finally, for those looking for traditional Spanish crafts and artwork, a visit to Artesanía El Sol is a must. This artisan shop features handmade pottery, traditional textiles, and other locally-made crafts. It's a great place to find unique and authentic gifts to bring back from your trip to Seville.

Whether you're looking for high-end antiques or unique souvenirs, you're sure to find something special in Seville.

Health and Safety

Emergency Medical Care in Seville
Seville has a range of medical facilities, including hospitals, clinics, and pharmacies, which offer emergency medical care to both locals and visitors.

In the case of a medical emergency, the first point of contact should be the emergency services. The Spanish emergency number is 112, which can be used to request medical, police, or fire services. The operators usually speak Spanish, but there are usually options to speak in other languages, including English.

If medical attention is required but it is not an emergency, it is recommended to visit a local medical center or clinic. The public healthcare system in Spain is accessible to all EU citizens with a valid European Health Insurance Card (EHIC), which can be obtained from your home country's healthcare authority. Non-EU citizens may need to pay for medical treatment, although travel insurance policies may cover this expense.

Private healthcare is also available in Seville, and it is generally quicker and more expensive than public healthcare. The cost of private medical care can vary depending on the type of treatment required.

Pharmacies, called "farmacias," can be found throughout Seville, and they offer a range of over-the-counter medications and prescription drugs. Pharmacists are trained to provide advice on minor ailments and can recommend appropriate treatments. Many pharmacies also offer emergency services outside of normal working hours.

It is recommended that travelers obtain comprehensive travel insurance before departing on their trip to Seville to ensure that they are covered for any medical emergencies that may arise during their stay.

Safety Tips for Traveling in Seville

Seville is generally a safe city for visitors, but it is always important to take precautions to ensure a safe and enjoyable trip. Here are some safety tips to keep in mind when traveling in Seville:

1. Be aware of your surroundings: As with any city, it is important to be aware of your surroundings, especially when traveling alone or at night. Keep your belongings close and avoid dark or isolated areas.

2. Use official taxis: If you need to take a taxi, make sure to use an official taxi service or app, and avoid taking unofficial taxis from the street.

3. Be cautious with valuables: Avoid carrying large amounts of cash or wearing expensive jewelry, as this can attract unwanted attention. Hide your valuables in a safe location, such as a hotel safe.

4. Use common sense: Use common sense when traveling in Seville. Don't leave your belongings unattended, be cautious of pickpockets, and avoid confrontations with strangers.

5. Follow local customs and laws: Seville is a relatively conservative city, and visitors should respect local customs and laws. Dress modestly when visiting churches or religious sites, and avoid public displays of affection.

6. Take care when crossing streets: Seville's narrow streets and alleys can be challenging to navigate, and drivers can be unpredictable. Take care when crossing streets, and always use designated crosswalks.

7. Be cautious in crowded areas: Seville is known for its lively festivals and events, which can attract large crowds. Be cautious in crowded areas and avoid getting separated from your group.

By following these safety tips, travelers can enjoy a safe and memorable trip to Seville. It is also recommended to stay up-to-date on local news and events and to register with your embassy or consulate in case of an emergency.

Emergency Contacts

It is always important to have access to emergency contacts when traveling to a new city. Here are some important emergency contacts for Seville:

1. General emergency number: 112. This number can be used for any emergency, including police, fire, or medical.

2. Tourist Police: (+34) 954 21 21 00. The Tourist Police is a specialized unit of the National Police that assist tourists in Seville.

3. Hospital emergency numbers: In case of a medical emergency, call 061 or 112.

4. Embassy or Consulate: If you are traveling as a foreigner, it is recommended to have the contact information for your embassy or consulate in case of an emergency.

5. Lost or stolen credit cards: If your credit cards are lost or stolen, contact your bank or credit card company immediately to report the incident and cancel your cards.

6. Lost or stolen passport: If your passport is lost or stolen, contact your embassy or consulate for assistance in obtaining a replacement.

7. Seville Tourist Office: (+34) 955 47 53 94. The Seville Tourist Office can provide information on tourist attractions, maps, and other helpful resources for visitors.

It is always a good idea to write down these emergency contacts and keep them with you while traveling in Seville.

Money Matters

Currency and Payment Options in Seville

The currency used in Seville and throughout Spain is the Euro (€). It is advisable to have some Euros on hand for small purchases and to avoid relying solely on credit or debit cards, which may not be accepted at some smaller establishments. ATMs are widely available throughout the city, but it is important to check with your bank about any fees or limitations for international withdrawals.

Credit and debit cards are widely accepted in Seville, especially in larger shops and restaurants. However, some smaller businesses, such as family-owned shops or street vendors, may only accept cash. It is always a good idea to have a mix of cash and cards and to carry smaller bills as many places may not be able to break larger denominations.

When paying with a credit or debit card, it is important to note that some businesses may require a minimum purchase amount before accepting payment by card. Additionally, some credit cards may charge foreign transaction fees, so it is important to check with your card issuer before traveling to Seville.

Tipping is not mandatory in Seville, but it is customary to round up the bill or leave a small amount of change as a gesture of appreciation for good service. In restaurants, a tip of 5-10% is typical for good service, but it is always up to the discretion of the customer.

Finally, it is important to note that Spain has implemented a Value Added Tax (VAT) system, known as IVA, which is included in the price of most goods and services. The standard VAT rate in Spain is currently 21%, but reduced rates of 10% and 4% apply to certain products, such as food and drink, books, and public transportation. Non-EU residents are eligible for a VAT refund on purchases over a certain amount, but it is necessary to follow certain procedures and provide the appropriate documentation at the time of purchase.

Money Mistakes to Avoid

When traveling to Seville, it's important to be mindful of your spending and budget accordingly. Here are some common money mistakes to avoid:

1. Not informing your bank or credit card company of your travel plans: Before leaving for Seville, make sure to notify your bank or credit card company of your travel plans to avoid any issues with card usage or security concerns.

2. Exchanging money at the airport or tourist areas: It's best to avoid exchanging money at the airport or in tourist areas as they tend to have higher exchange rates and fees. Instead, withdraw money from an ATM or exchange money at a local bank.

3. Overusing credit cards: While credit cards can be convenient, it's important not to rely solely on them. Some businesses in Seville

may only accept cash, so it's best to have some euros on hand.

4. Falling for tourist traps: Tourist traps can be tempting, but they can also be overpriced and offer lower-quality products or services. Do your research and ask locals for recommendations to avoid falling for tourist traps.

5. Ignoring currency exchange rates: Make sure to keep an eye on currency exchange rates to ensure you're getting the best value for your money. Consider using a currency converter app or website to stay informed.

6. Not budgeting properly: It's important to budget and plan your spending before arriving in Seville to avoid overspending and running out of money. Consider setting a daily spending limit and sticking to it.

7. Forgetting to check for hidden fees: Some businesses may have hidden fees such as

service charges or additional taxes, so make sure to check the fine print before making a purchase.

By avoiding these common money mistakes, you can enjoy your trip to Seville without any financial stress or surprises.

Tips for managing money and navigating local currency exchange

Managing money and navigating local currency exchange can be a challenge. However, with some helpful tips, you can ensure that you have enough money to enjoy your trip and avoid unnecessary expenses. Here are some tips for managing money and navigating local currency exchange in Seville:

1. Get Familiar with the Euro: Spain uses the Euro as its official currency. Before you arrive in Seville, make sure to familiarize

yourself with the currency, including its denominations and exchange rate. This will make it easier for you to manage your money while traveling.

2. Bring Cash and Cards: While credit and debit cards are widely accepted in Seville, it's a good idea to bring some cash with you as well. Make sure to exchange your money at a reputable currency exchange office or bank to avoid being ripped off by high exchange rates.

3. Use ATMs: ATMs are widely available in Seville, and they offer a convenient way to withdraw cash when you need it. However, be aware of transaction fees and currency conversion fees that may apply when using an ATM abroad.

4. Avoid Currency Exchange Kiosks: While currency exchange kiosks may seem like a convenient option, they often charge high

exchange rates and hidden fees. Instead, use a bank or currency exchange office for the best rates.

5. Notify Your Bank and Credit Card Companies: Before traveling to Seville, make sure to notify your bank and credit card companies of your travel plans. This will prevent your cards from being blocked due to suspicious activity while you're abroad.

6. Don't Keep All Your Money in One Place: When traveling, it's always a good idea to keep your money in different places to avoid losing all your funds in case of theft or loss. Keep some cash and a credit card in your wallet, and leave the rest in a safe place in your hotel room.

7. Be Cautious of Pickpockets: Like many popular tourist destinations, Seville has its fair share of pickpockets. Keep your wallet

and valuables in a secure place, and be aware of your surroundings in crowded areas.

By following these tips, you can ensure that you have enough money to enjoy your trip and avoid unnecessary expenses.

Communications

Wi-Fi and Internet Access in Seville

When traveling, staying connected to the internet is important, whether it's for work or for staying in touch with family and friends. Fortunately, there are many options available for Wi-Fi and internet access in Seville.

Hotels and Accommodations: Most hotels and accommodations in Seville offer Wi-Fi to their guests free of charge. However, some may charge for higher speeds or access beyond a certain data limit. It's best to check with your hotel ahead of time to ensure that Wi-Fi is available and any potential fees that may be associated with it.

Coffee Shops and Cafés: Many coffee shops and cafes in Seville offer free Wi-Fi to customers. Some popular options include Starbucks, Costa Coffee, and Caffé di Fiore. Additionally, many local cafes and bakeries also offer free Wi-Fi, so it's worth exploring your surroundings to find a cozy spot to work or catch up on emails.

Public Wi-Fi: Seville offers free public Wi-Fi in some areas of the city, including in the Plaza Nueva and along the banks of the Guadalquivir River. To connect, simply search for the "SevillaWifi" network on your device, and follow the prompts to connect. However, it's important to note that public Wi-Fi can be less secure than other options, so it's best to avoid sensitive activities such as online banking or shopping while connected to a public network.

SIM Cards and Mobile Data: For travelers who need more reliable internet access or plan on staying in Seville for an extended period, purchasing a local SIM card or a mobile data plan may be a better option. SIM cards can be purchased from mobile phone shops and kiosks throughout the city, and plans can be tailored to fit a variety of needs and budgets. Some of the major mobile carriers in Spain include Movistar, Vodafone, and Orange.

Portable Wi-Fi Devices: Another option for internet access in Seville is to rent or purchase a portable Wi-Fi device. These devices allow you to connect multiple devices to the internet simultaneously and are a good option for travelers who need to stay connected while on the go. Portable Wi-Fi devices can be rented from a variety of companies online or in person in Seville, such as Travelers Wifi.

Using Mobile Phones in Seville

Using a mobile phone in Seville is convenient, as there is widespread mobile network coverage and a variety of mobile service providers available. However, there are some important things to keep in mind when using your phone in Seville.

If you are traveling from outside the European Union, you may need to check with your mobile service provider to ensure that your phone is compatible with European networks. You may also need to activate international roaming services to avoid excessive roaming charges.

Once you arrive in Seville, you can purchase a prepaid SIM card from any mobile phone store or kiosk. These SIM cards are widely available and relatively inexpensive, and they offer a convenient way to stay connected while traveling in Seville. Most mobile service providers in Seville offer prepaid SIM cards that come with a certain amount of calling time, text messages, and mobile data.

Another option for using your mobile phone in Seville is to connect to Wi-Fi hotspots. Many cafes, restaurants, and public places in Seville offer free Wi-Fi access to their customers, and there are also several public Wi-Fi hotspots available throughout the city. However, it's important to be cautious when using public Wi-Fi, as these networks can be vulnerable to security breaches and data theft.

If you plan to use your mobile phone extensively while in Seville, it's a good idea to download a map or navigation app to help you get around. Google Maps and other popular navigation apps can be accessed offline, which means you don't need an active mobile data connection to use them. This can be especially useful if you are traveling in areas with limited mobile network coverage.

When using your mobile phone in Seville, it's important to be aware of your surroundings and keep your phone secure at all times. Petty theft, including mobile phone theft, is a common problem in crowded tourist areas, so it's important to keep your phone in a secure place and be cautious when using it in public.

Power and Adapters for Electronic Devices

It is important to know what kind of power outlets are used in the country and what kind of adapters or converters you may need for your electronic devices. Here is what you need to know about the power supply in Seville, the type of plugs and sockets used, and tips on how to stay connected during your trip.

The first thing you should know is that Spain uses a 230V/50Hz electrical system, which is different from the system used in North America and some other parts of the world. If you are traveling from a country with a different voltage or frequency, you will need to bring a voltage converter or transformer to avoid damaging your electronic devices.

The second thing to consider is the type of plugs and sockets used in Spain. Spain uses Type C and Type F plugs, which have two round pins and two round pins with a grounding hole, respectively. If your devices have plugs that are not compatible with these types, you will need a plug adapter.

It is important to note that some hotels and other accommodations in Seville may provide adapters or converters for their guests. However, it is always a good idea to bring your own to avoid any potential problems.

Final thoughts on Seville as a travel destination

Seville is a beautiful and culturally rich destination that has something to offer every type of traveler. From historic landmarks and architectural marvels to delicious food and vibrant nightlife, Seville is a city that should be on every traveler's bucket list.

One of the best things about Seville is that it offers a luxurious experience even on a budget, making it an ideal destination for those looking to save some money while still enjoying a high-end vacation. With a wide range of accommodation options, from budget-friendly hostels to luxury hotels, and a vibrant culinary scene that caters to all budgets, Seville has everything you need for a memorable trip.

When it comes to transportation, Seville's public transport system is efficient and affordable, making it easy to navigate the city's narrow streets and alleys. And with its warm Mediterranean climate, Seville is a year-round destination that is perfect for both summer and winter travel.

Finally, Seville's rich cultural heritage and friendly locals make it a great destination for immersing yourself in the local customs and traditions. Whether you're interested in flamenco dancing, exploring the city's historic sites, or simply relaxing and enjoying the laid-back vibe of this beautiful city, Seville is a destination that should not be missed.

In conclusion, Seville is a travel destination that offers a perfect blend of history, culture, food, and nightlife, making it a great place to visit for travelers of all ages and interests. So start planning your trip to Seville today and get ready to experience the best of what this beautiful city has to offer!